T0078144

The HEART OF A WORSHIPER

Kateryann Johnson, CPA, CGMA, CFF

authorHOUSE®

AuthorHouse™
1663 Liberty Drive
Bloomington, IN 47403
www.authorhouse.com
Phone: 1 (800) 839-8640

Edited by Pastor Peter Lanya

Published by AuthorHouse 01/25/2017

ISBN: 978-1-5246-5893-9 (sc)
ISBN: 978-1-5246-5892-2 (e)

Print information available on the last page.

Time of Worship and Exhortation

I want to start this book off with a time of praise and worship. Right where you are, please lift your hands as an evening sacrifice to the king of Kings. Open up your mouth and begin to worship. Begin to offer the fruit of your lips. We are the only beings that can bless the Lord with the fruit of our lips. Go ahead and join me in a time of worship!

Lord, You are Mighty, Faithful and a strong Deliverer.

You are great and greatly to be praised.

Search me O God and know my heart today. See if there be any contrary way in me. Please remove from me all that takes me out of Your divine will in the name of Jesus. Please purify my heart for worship.

You are simply the Great I Am! As Psalm 46:1 declares You are our Refuge and Strength, a very present help in trouble. Therefore, we will not fear.

There is none like You. I have searched all over and found that there is none like You.

Let my worship come up to You as a sweet smelling savor.

Let my worship be a testimony to some lost soul that they may come to know You as Lord and Saviour.

Lord, let my worship flow to You. I love You more than anything. You are my all and all!

I set you on the highest plain because You are God and besides You there is none other. Amen!

Child of God, continue to worship your God is Spirit and in truth. Live a life of worship. Every thought of God today, give Him worship and praise. He is so worthy and the devil is defeated in Jesus name.

Continue to enjoy the best day ever, for it is your portion!

Some Beautiful Psalms For A Worshiper

From the rising of the sun to the going down of the same, the name of the Lord is worthy of praise. Psalm 113:3

He that dwell in the secret place of the Most High shall abide under the shadow of the Almighty. Psalm 91:1

Enter His Gates with Thanksgiving and into His courts with praise and worship. Psalm 100:4

Clap your hands all ye people and shout unto God with a voice of triumph. Psalm 47:1

O Lord, our Lord, how excellent is Your name in all the earth, You who set Your glory above the heavens. Out of the mouths of babes and infants thou has ordained praise, because of your enemies, That you may silence the enemy and the avenger. Psalm 8:1-2

Contents

My Inspiration and Dedication

I have heartfelt persuasion to call people into true worship. God loves worship and seeks people who will worship him in spirit and truth.

It is my humble plea to inspire worship leaders, church leaders and the entire congregation to know what worship is and do it in the right way. This is the way to see God's presence, His manifestations and the only onslaught against the schemes of the enemy.

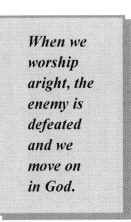

When we worship aright, the enemy is defeated and we move on in God.

When we worship, the enemy is defeated and we move on in God.

It has been my prayer and desires, as I write this book, to enlighten the church. I believe, through this book, God will open the hearts of His people to learn some basic things that we have taken for granted.

I pray that you will be one of the many persons who will benefit from this book.

I dedicate this book to God and my two handsome sons who I affectionately call SJ and K'Juan.

Introduction

Worship is for the spiritually mature. It is for the spiritually hungry. The message of worship is not some hidden truth reserved only for the seasonal saints of the deeper life. It is a street lived message that will challenge the imagination of even the most hardened among humanity. God is looking for worshipers and it is not difficult to become one of them. Worship is not some kind of acquired skill that commonly be learned after years of religious training. It is actually the most natural response of God's creation to his Master and Creator.

> *When Praise and Worship leaders learn to maximize this fully, then we will begin to see the witness power of worship.*

We can now see that worship through evangelism is very powerful, but one must be careful because some have made evangelism the goal of worship and turned worship into a camp meeting.

It is beautiful to seek God without any other motives. It moves people to see that there are individuals who do worship God, who really do love God with all their heart, soul, mind and strength. Worship becomes a very powerful testimonial of hope and love to a world living on the edge of despair.

When Praise and Worship leaders learn to maximize this fully, then we will begin to see the witness power of worship. I believe we will see an increasing number of people converted to the Lord through the witness of wholehearted Christian worship.

God designed worship to witness and it will witness.

God intended for seekers to observe our worship and become worshipers. "All the nations you have made will come and worship before you, O Lord, and will bring glory to your name". Ps 86:9

There seems to be a wide spread of ignorance regarding what Christian worship actually is. In a study involving the same regular church goers who responded to the "satisfaction" question found an alarming discrepancy between the understanding worship and the Biblical teaching of worship.

When we asked the same church attendee to define the meaning of worship for us, we learned that 36% provided a reasonable assessment of what worship means, 25% provided answers that were too generic to evaluate, 39% offered explanations that were clearly erroneous. Thus, a substantial proportion of the worship population appears to be unclear about what it is they venture to the church to accomplish each weekend. This in turn, calls into question the values or validity of having satisfied people' expectation regarding a worship experience.

The most significant benefit of a worship service is connecting with God. It really does not matter how interesting the celebrity interviews, how captivating the drama, how stunning the soloist, or how relevant the message. When personal interaction with God is absent, church loses much of its appeal.

It is of this essence that I try to lay bare what is worship, the ingredients of worship and how the church can move from casual worship to an encounter with God where people's lives are changed and transformed by His presence.

In this environment, carnality is destroyed, shallowness of faith dies and people move into higher dimension of seeing the glory of God. They desire God more and thirst for His presence. It ignites in them the passion to be with the Lord. Remember, God's presence makes life colorful and easy to manage because His wisdom, strength and power are enough to keep you aloft over the works of the devil and the systems of the world.

Get set for an encounter as you go deeper into true worship. I believe your life won't be the same again.

> *Remember God's presence makes life colorful and easy to manage because His wisdom, strength and power are enough to keep you aloft over the works of the devil and the systems of the world.*

Chapter 1

What is Worship?

Worship is the act and attitude of wholeheartedly giving ourselves to God—spirit, soul and body. Worship is simply the expression of our love for God, which Jesus said should involve all our hearts, mind and physical strength.

And you shall love the LORD your God with all your heart, with all your soul, with all your mind, and with all your strength. This *is* the first commandment—NKJV, Mark 12:30

Man is a worshiper whether they acknowledge it or not. Everybody worships. Your job, money, possession, a movie, TV show or a recording are forms of worship; they even call them their idols. Some of us worship God.

Regardless of what is worshipped, everyone worships something. The amazing thing here is that many people do not even recognize what it is they are worshipping because they do not have a clear idea of what worship means.

Worship comes from the old English word *''worthship 'which means to ascribe worth unto'*. The essential idea is that whatever it is that you value most highly or place the greatest worth upon is what you worship.

To worship is to bow down to or before. It is rendered paying homage to God. It is sinful (idolatry) to render homage to any created being (Exodus 34:14; Isaiah 2:8). Such worship was refused by Peter (Acts 10:25,26) and by an angel (Revelation 22:8,9).

Worship also means "Honor, reverence, homage, in thought, feeling, or act, paid to men, angels, or other "spiritual" beings, and figuratively to other entities, ideas, powers or qualities, but specifically and supremely to Deity.

The principal Old Testament word is "shachah", "depress," "bow down," "prostrate" (Hithpael), as in Exodus 4:31, "bowed their heads and worshipped"; so in 94 other places. The context determines more or less clearly whether the physical act or the volitional or emotional idea is intended. The word is applied to acts of reverence to human superiors as well as supernatural.

The Old Testament idea is therefore the reverential attitude of mind or body or both, combined with the more generic notions of religions adoration, obedience and service.

According to the International Standard Bible, the principal New Testament word (59 times) is "proskuneo", "kiss (the hand or the ground) toward," hence, often in the oriental fashion bowing prostrate

New Testament worship was characterized by a joy and thanksgiving because of God's gracious redemption in Christ. This early Christian worship focused on

Worship may also mean "Honor, reverence, homage, in thought, feeling, or act, paid to men, angels, or other "spiritual" beings, and figuratively to other entities, ideas, powers or qualities, but specifically and supremely to Deity.

God's saving work in Jesus Christ. True worship was that which occurred under the inspiration of God's Spirit (John 4:23-24; Philippians 3:3).

Psalms 115:1-8, says *"Not to us, O LORD, not to us but to your name be the glory, because of your love and faithfulness.*

Why do the nations say, "Where is their God?" Our God is in heaven; he does whatever pleases him.

But their idols are silver and gold, made by the hands of men.

They have mouths, but cannot speak, eyes, but they cannot see; they have ears, but cannot hear, noses, but they cannot smell; they have hands, but cannot feel, feet, but they cannot walk; nor can they utter a sound with their throats.

Those who make them will be like them, and so will all who trust in them". (NIV)

The psalmist is talking about idolatry and the inadequacy of these idol gods that the heathen were worshipping.

Please note this statement, *"You become like the God (god) you worship".*

Your worship determines what flows from your life. Our highest attainment comes through glorifying Him who is worthy of all glory.

3

The gods that are worshipped begin to manifest their attributes in the worshiper. So you have to be careful with what you worship. Worship is spiritual, it affects your heart. But the fulfillment of our hearts comes as a direct result of our approaching God and coming to know Him. Some very significant issues are determined by our worship.

(i) We bring our hearts into alignment with whatever we worship.

(ii) Worship deals with whom you seek and the seeking has to be with what you pursue and to what you submit.

(iii) The object of my worship becomes the guiding force of my life.

(iv) Worship determines what you will discover.

Proverbs 16:4 says, *'he who follows another god will discover what he provides but ultimately there is no other fulfillment for that emptiness''*

(v) Your worship determines what flows from your life. Our highest attainment comes through glorifying Him who is worthy of all glory.

Finding a relationship with God is to want to glorify Him and worship leads us along that path. When we bring an offering and come before Him, then worship is excellently done. The Bible says, ***"Worship the Lord in the beauty of Holiness.***

THE CALL TO WORSHIP

Man is a creature of worship. That is why we should know who the object of our worship is. As a matter of fact, people direct their worship to other things to resemble God but they are idols. If we want to see impact in our worship, the following demands should be put in place.

Abraham was called the father of faith after his response to the call of worship. Everybody is called to be a worshiper.

1. We will be called into a new place in Him. There is no settlement in God. Revelation of God should make us climb the ladder of worship. Don't settle in your traditions and customs and deceive yourself that is all there is in worship. God is progressive. He wants you to change. Keep moving and you would see God in a new way.

2. We are called to surrender those things that are at the heart of our ambitions and dreams. The true nature of God is never to destroy what He created us to be, but to release in us what has always been His highest intention. God's nature had to take away Abraham's fears. As a result, he saw a fresh revelation of God's goodness, mercy and grace.

Obedience to our call to worship brings us fresh discovery and further discovery of God's nature and His provision. Abraham saw a new face of the nature of God "and he called that place Jehovah Jireh.

Genesis 22:13-14—"*Then Abraham lifted his eyes and looked, and there behind him was a ram caught in a thicket by its horns. So Abraham went and took the ram, and offered it up for a burnt offering instead of his son. 14 And Abraham called the name of the

place, The-LORD-Will-Provide; as it is said to this day, "In the Mount of the LORD it shall be provided." (NKJV)

Abraham was called the father of faith after his response to the call of worship. Everybody is called to be a worshiper. **Genesis 22:15-18-** tells us that the Lord blessed Abraham in response to his faithfulness. We, likewise, find that we are blessed in response to answering the call to worship. We soon find that the very things that we were afraid of losing are the things that the Lord promotes to multiply and bless us abundantly.

THE ATTRIBUTES OF GOD THAT TRIGGERS WORSHIP

The significance of worship is that we become like the God we worship. The following attributes of God will enhance your worship. You need revelation to worship God in spirit and in truth

The Lord is Eternal – this means He embraces all time.

God is Almighty – obviously this means there are no restrictions to His power. The lord created and sustains the entire universe by the word of His power.

He is Omnipresent- That simply means that God is everywhere.

Omniscient- He is all knowing

He is Holy – means that God can never be less than who He is.

THE BEAUTY OF WORSHIP

The beauty of worship should flow out of your heart (John 4:24). Worship is intended to cultivate wholeness and order that becomes beauty in our lives. It is our responsibility to worship Him. In worship, there is holiness and beauty. (Isaiah 6).

Worship is to prepare us for the next stage of life no matter where we are currently. Our inadequacy and weakness is swallowed up in true worship. In the beauty of worship, we come and see His awesome holiness.

God's holiness does not and would not deny us access to him, but is intended to purify out things that make us inadequate and intimidate us from fulfilling destiny. His presence is what we need in life.

Exodus 33:12-23--''*Moses said to the LORD, "You have been telling me, 'Lead these people,' but you have not let me know whom you will send with me. You have said, 'I know you by name and you have found favor with me.' 13 If you are pleased with me, teach me your ways so I may know you and continue to find favor with you. Remember that this nation is your people."*

The LORD replied, "My Presence will go with you, and I will give you rest." Then Moses said to him, "If your Presence does not go with us, do not send us up from here. 16 How will anyone know that you are pleased with me and with your people unless you go with us? What else will distinguish me and your people from all the other people on the face of the earth?"

And the LORD said to Moses, "I will do the very thing you have asked, because I am pleased with you and I know you by name."

Then Moses said, "Now show me your glory."

And the LORD said, "I will cause all my goodness to pass in front of you, and I will proclaim my name, the LORD, in your presence. I will have mercy on whom I will have mercy, and I will have compassion on whom I will have compassion. But," he said, "you cannot see my face, for no one may see me and live."

Then the LORD said, "There is a place near me where you may stand on a rock. 22 When my glory passes by, I will put you in a cleft in the rock and cover you with my hand until I have passed by. 23 Then I will remove my hand and you will see my back; but my face must not be seen." (NIV)

God is spirit and those who worship Him must worship in spirit and in truth (John 4:24). This simply means that every worshiper should allow the work of His spirit in their lives. True worship comes by the Spirit of God. That is why Jesus told the disciples to wait for the empowerment of the Spirit. Filling by the Spirit is not a one day event and settle there, thinking there is nothing else. We should desire continuous baptism of the Spirit to worship God in new dimensions. Those who see worship as a burden and tiresome are doing it by their carnal flesh. My friend, it is not so. The fullness of worship comes by the Holy Spirit.

God is spirit and those who worship Him must worship in spirit and in truth (John 4:24).

Our worship can become a vibrant encounter when we are connected to the Father. Time won't be an issue. Moses enjoyed God's presence. That is the beauty of worship. His presence is what makes the whole difference. The fullness of worship was manifested with the first church. We see the Holy Spirit coming with power upon the disciples. When you are filled with Spirit of God, worship becomes the natural result. Worshiping

God is simply telling about who God is and His wonderful works after you are filled by the Holy Spirit. The fullness of the spirit of God in us always creates hunger to seek Him. Anything bothering us is answered by the teaching of the Word because it is fresh through worship. God comes home when we worship Him and answers our bothering questions.

Spirit filled worship whether it is with understanding or utterance in your native language or with spiritual language is edifying and satisfies the hungry heart.

John 7:37-39--*"On the last day, that great day of the feast, Jesus stood and cried out, saying, "If anyone thirsts, let him come to Me and drink. 38 He who believes in Me, as the Scripture has said, out of his heart will flow rivers of living water." But this He spoke concerning the Spirit, whom those believing in Him would receive; for the Holy Spirit was not yet given, because Jesus was not yet glorified"(NKJV)*

Those who are led by the spirit of God are the true sons of God (Romans 8:14).

I Corinthians 14:17 says, when you worship in the Spirit, you are giving thanks to God also. The Lord loves a grateful person.

Chapter 2

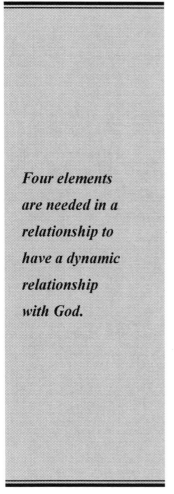

Worship Centered in Christ

Four elements are needed in a relationship to have a dynamic relationship with God.

Interaction coupled with participation is an ongoing dialogue of both words and songs. Worship is a dialogue using a language both of us can understand – God and the worshiper.

Four elements are needed in a relationship to have a dynamic relationship with God.

The four elements are nearness, knowledge, vulnerability, and interaction.

Nearness- a sense of God's presence.

Psalms 139:7-8--Where can I go from Your Spirit?
Or where can I flee from Your presence?
If I ascend into heaven, You are there;
If I make my bed in hell, behold, You are there--NKJV

God's universal presence or omnipresence is a marvelous fact of life. God promises to be manifested in a special way as we worship together.

He inhabits the praises of His people. He dwells or resides there.

There is a blessing in God's presence.

We serve a self- revealing God. The process of worship is all well and good, but the fact that God waits for us to become aware of His presence does explain why 34% of church goers say they never experience God's presence in a church and another 27% say they rarely experience God's presence or they are not sure. God's presence is all around, but His revealed manifested presence is when we become aware of His presence.

Think about the people with whom you are very close to. Perhaps you are with your best college buddy or maybe it is your spouse. Whether you realize it or not, your ongoing relationship with this person depends on the same four basic elements.

Nearness, Knowledge, Vulnerability, and Interaction are all essential elements in worship. These elements have fostered increased intimacy over many months and years and thus, they are the reason this relationship has become fulfilling and significant. It is a lifestyle and not just a Sunday morning experience.

Nearness - we spend time in the other person's presence. We spend time with God through worship and prayer.

Knowledge –we get to know who the other person is. This is what makes that person different from all other individuals we get to know. We get to know God in worship because He speaks to us. We also know Him through the written word.

Vulnerability-we risk rejection and allow ourselves to become known. We may be rejected by man but we will never be rejected by God. So, it is okay to be vulnerable and broken in the presence of the Almighty God. He will take good care of you.

Interaction is how often or how frequent partners connect in whatever form or fashion.

God went down in the cool of the day to meet with Adam. He desires to commune with mankind. He said in the book of Revelation that we were created for His pleasure. The book of Genesis clearly informs us that God loves interaction with man, His prize creation.

Revelations 4:11--"You are worthy, O Lord, to receive glory and honor and power; for You created all things, and by Your will they exist* and were created."-NKJV

"Worship Evangelism" Essentials

The product of the church is relationship with God, not religion.

If seekers are going to be attracted to our worship and if we hope to keep believers coming back, we need churches where worship is in existence and something is happening. The question is what does it really take for something to happen in worship? Beyond anything and everything, we must move beyond dress or the way we look on Sunday morning, which is superficial. The important thing is whether the heart is dressed for worship.

Psalms 24:3-4 says, "Who shall ascend in the hill of the Lord, who shall stand in

God went down in the cool of the day to meet with Adam. He desires to commune with mankind. He said in the book of Revelation that we were created for His pleasure.

Worship is the gospel in motion. Seekers not only hear the truth about God but observe the "Gospel in Motion", through believers interacting with God through Christ.

His holy place. He that have clean hands and a pure heart..."*

The worship environment worth coming into is worship that evidences a dynamic relationship with God. However, in the best relationships, there is always something happening. They are never static or boring.

The Seeker as Worshiper

Another valid concern among those opposed to inviting seekers into worship is that somehow the seeker's presence in the worship experience may identify him or her as a worshiper. But can a seeker actually worship? Scripture infers that an unbeliever cannot worship God until he or she has a relationship with God through Jesus Christ. In John 4:23-24, Jesus makes it clear that those who would worship God must do so in Spirit and in truth. Yes, we can all praise. For the Bible says in Psalms, "… let everything that have breath praise the Lord." We can all give thanks also because all through the scriptures, we are admonished to give thanks to Almighty God.

Worship, on the other hand, is different. It calls for relationship with God and must be done in Spirit and truth. God wants a clean vessel where love abounds because God is love. That is why sins of the heart block worship and its potential impact on an individual or even the seekers around them.

Yes, worship is heard, but it is experienced even more, more than it is heard. Worship is the gospel in motion. Seekers not only hear the truth about God, but observe the "Gospel in Motion", through believers interacting with God through Christ. Good worship is just by its nature and essence evangelistic. So even though our worship is definitely focused on Christians worshipping, I believe wholeheartedly that there is an evangelistic aspect there.

Worship is not design primarily with unbelievers in mind, but the design ultimately impacts the unbeliever. Everything we do should be a sensitive and understandable to unbelievers as much as possible. The church must be about evangelism, but it also must be about worship.

Chapter 3

Worship and Evangelism: Do they go together?

Worshipers do not just enjoy God's wonderful presence for themselves. They call others to join them there through faith in Christ. And those of you who want to see the world come to Christ, just call men and women to believe, call them to worship.

It's time for worship leaders to learn the art of calling unbelievers to Christ through worship.

We should work to make our church a "Seeker Sensitive" congregation where visitors would feel welcome. Visitors should be assured of an abbreviated, yet quality time of worship followed by a culturally relevant message.

We cannot 'conjure' God's manifest presence into being. God's self revelation is not automatic. James 4:8 is clear "come near to God and He will come near to you".

There is a pre-requisite.

What is Worship Evangelism?

Worship Evangelism is defined into two profound but simple phrases,

1. "Wholehearted worshipers calling the whole world to the whole hearted worship of God…

2. and the fusion of the power of God's presence with the power of the gospel.

> *Worship evangelism happens when we allow worship to be what it was meant to be "a resource for incomplete and broken mankind to find completion and wholeness in His presence.*

Worship evangelism happens when we allow worship to be what it was meant to be. It is a resource for incomplete and broken mankind to find completion and wholeness in His presence. It happens when we "let God out of the box". It is time to put these two words, "Worship and Evangelism" together without apology.

We pursue God because and only because He has first loved us. He is God and besides Him there is no other. Jesus says, "No one can come to me unless the Father who sent me draws him" (John 6:44). His unfailing, infallible love draws us.

We must allow our worship to witness. Today, lost people have turned a deaf ear to Christianity, but their hearts are being drawn to spiritual things. Worship such as that in the Philippian jail - exaltation of God incarnate and presence with God's people –is what seekers really need to see in our churches. When Paul and Silas began to worship, conversion took place in those hands.

We may not want worship to witness because we may not believe it can witness. We must worship in truth. Obviously, a seeker is still being drawn to the truth. The Bible declares, "I seek such that will worship in Spirit and in truth." Worship is a spiritual act and can only be understood in the spirit. The truth is the power the worshiper posses in a mode of worship.

Nevertheless, by the Spirit of God, he or she is drawn and the things of God are revealed. The unbeliever in whom God is working with is therefore capable of at least some spiritual understanding and discernment. For example, before his conversion, Pharisee Nicodemus was able to discern by the Holy Spirit that Jesus had come from God. (John 3:1-2)

In theological terms, this truth is called "preeminent grace". Basically, it means that before anyone can seek God, God first seeks him or her. Tozer describes it this way, "Before a sinful man can think a right thought of God, there must have been a work of enlightenment done within him….the secret cause of all desiring, seeking and praying."

What is Paul saying in 1 Corinthians 14:23-25 about worship?

Being prophetic, we speak forth truth of God in our worship service, as we proclaim who Jesus is and what He's done. And as we are doing that, people say, "God is in this place". God inhabits the praises of His people, because the

Firstly, it happens as unbelievers hear the truth about God whether through worship songs, prayer, communion, baptism, scripture, testimonies, dramas and so on.

Spirit of God is in the worship and the doctrine taught is understood clearly.

How does worship evangelism happens? How does evangelism take place in service that is fully worship?

It happens in 2 ways. Firstly, it happens as unbelievers hear the truth about God whether through worship songs, prayer, communion, baptism, scripture, testimonies, dramas and so on.

Secondly and more importantly, it takes place as they observe the real relationship between worshipers and God.

The concept is witness in your worship. Do you remember what happened in the jail? In Acts 16, we see how God used worship to evangelize unbelievers in a Philippians jail.

"About midnight Paul and Silas were praying and singing hymns to God, and the other prisoners were listening to them.

"Then he called for a light, ran in, and fell down trembling before Paul and Silas. 30 And he brought them out and said,"Sirs, what must I do to be saved?"

So they said,"Believe on the Lord Jesus Christ, and you will be saved, you and your household." 32 Then they spoke the word of the Lord to him and to all who were in his house--Acts 16:25-32, NKJV

Here, we read of two innocent men bleeding from beatings and chained to their cells but yet, they worshiped. No wonder the other prisoners were listening instead of jeering. There was something awesome going on in the cell! These men worshiped with their lives and their lips and Christ was obviously present in their praise.

There was no stadium here; there were no appeals for repentance. Paul and Silas did not look and focus on their present condition. They just worshipped!

The point is, evangelism comes in many shapes and sizes. Millions of people around the world have come to Jesus Christ through traditional rallies and crusades. However, seekers also come to know Christ in other ways and one of those ways is worship.

A distinct advantage of witnessing through worship service is that worship services happen every week. Seekers can keep coming to experience God's presence, to hear about Jesus and witness Jesus in action.

We must realize that Evangelism through worship is one of the most powerful tools for winning souls and membership. Worship is not selfish and the most pure way of expressing your love for God. People are simply responding genuinely.

This deals with inviting unbelievers to believe and become aware of the presence of God.

We wanted it to be like 1 Corinthians 14:22 kind of worship where the unbeliever looks around and say, "Hey, God's here! A time whereby we invite God to invade our space and actually engage people with Him.

Worship and Effectiveness

Effective worship should inspire more worship, not less. This truth is being strangely ignored. It is as if worship and especially prepackaged worship, is immune to accountability.

We must realize that Evangelism through worship is one of the most powerful tools for winning souls and membership. Worship is not selfish and is the most pure way of expressing your love for God.

Unfortunately, many of us as pastors and church leaders are unaware that people are becoming dissatisfied, particularly in churches with attendance of a thousand or more. Our worship centre looks full every Sunday. The numbers are up or at least being maintained. Yet on any given Sunday only about 50% of the people are returnees from the previous Sunday. Even if we are aware, the sanctuary's front door has now become a revolving door. We ignore this fact as long as more people seem to be coming in than going out.

We must be concerned because the number of people leaving is starting to exceed the number of people coming in.

Worship creates influence. Only those who encounter God in His presence can influence people in the right way. The same principle applies in the negative. Those appear in presence of the devil influences people negatively. The witch-doctors, magicians and so many others have negative influence. The church can receive its influence from God's presence. We need more of His presence than anything else.

Chapter 4

Difficulties in Leading Worship

Where people interact, there's bound to be frictions, misunderstanding and all sorts of problems. Our strength, hope and direction come from the Lord who deserves all the worship.

There are difficulties in leading worship. We cannot dig our heads in the sand and pretend there are none. Wherever people interact, there is bound to be frictions, misunderstanding and all sorts of problems. Our strength, hope and direction come from the Lord who deserves all the worship. The Lord knows our inadequacies, limitations and boundaries. He comes in to help at the time of need.

That is why it will help the congregation open their hearts to God's love.

Worship leaders must understand the theology in ruff situations.

Worship leaders cannot always read someone except by the expression on his or her countenance. Simply, because someone can enjoy worship service, but it still not be evident on their face.

Do not seek to focus on the expression on the congregation; seek for the face of God. Once worship is sincerely from the heart and not just an act, ministry becomes easier.

Difficulties in Leading Worship

Let us look at these major difficulties in leading worship.

1. The reason some may not show expression outward is because of the natural tendency of people to be timid or shy in public gathering, unless it is socially acceptable to be enthusiastic.

2. Individuals will be even more intimidated if they do not know anyone in church.

3. If the worship leader does not understand these social ramifications in worship, they will build an attitude against the people who are unresponsive.

4. If you as a worship leader are experiencing a challenge, then flow through the prophetic anointing of the Holy Spirit.

The way forward

The worship of God starts with the individual giving reverence to God and giving him true honor due to him as He has commanded, and not as we wish to do it.

Psalm 100: 3-4 says, *"Know that the Lord is God, it is He who made us, and we are His; we are his people, the sheep of His pasture."*

The climax is when we gather together as group of worshipers to express our gratitude and thanksgiving to God Almighty for His faithfulness, (Psalm 81:1-3). Of course, there will be designated group of people who will lead in these times in our various churches. This group of people are called of God for this service in the house of God. They are specially skilled or trained in the act of skillful worship to God.

These selected individuals (Worship leaders) must;

Psalm 100: 3-4 says, *"Know that the Lord is God, it is He who made us, and we are His; we are his people, the sheep of His pasture."*

(i) Be identified with God.

(ii) Accept Him as their Lord, Master and Saviour.

(iii) Prepared to show forth His glory in every area of their lives.

(iv) Called of God for this service.

(v) Know the Word of God in-depth so as to keep within the boundaries of worship.

(vi) Led of the Spirit of God and understands the Lord deserves worship and so the Spirit helps to reach that realm of true worship-(John 4:24).

Chapter 5

The Art of Exhortation

The word Exhort in Greek is "Patakaleo" – to urge one to pursue some course of conduct. This is in retrospective and having to do with trial experienced.

When to use Exhortation?

Use exhortation in worship when reaching a crescendo or climax.

Exhortation is properly expressed under a prophetic anointing.

Too much exhortation can be dangerous. It will help people to become aware of their laziness and inspire the worship leader to escalate their enthusiasm. In this case, most people abuse it and have become a preacher.

During times of Exhortation, one should stand up, speak up, shut up and do not over do it.

The word Exhort in Greek is "Patakaleo" – to urge one to pursue some course of conduct.

The Leaders Musical Expertise

It was David's skill that brought him to the attention of Saul. Therefore, we should aspire to develop our musical expertise.

1. Have the desire to develop and grow from where you are.

2. Read and meditate God's word.

3. Grow and develop in conducting abilities.

4. Be prayerful to receive the anointing to maintain worship. Prayer is intimacy with the Lord in the secret place where our spirit is charged, rejuvenated and empowered to function effectively.

5. Consistency in practice. Whatever you practice, you will improve day by day. Music should be part of you.

The Art of Exhortation

This is where the congregation is led to a place of readiness.

The people do not need whipping, they have been battered all day. Simply speak to their Spirit man as the Holy Spirit gives utterance.

Prophetic Exhortation- this is why the leader is able to know what song he or she would need to use according to the flow of the atmosphere.

Exhortation is not manipulation; it falls into the area of persuasion.

*In 2 Corinthians 8:16-17 it says, "But thanks be to God who puts the same earnest care for you into the heart of Titus. For he not only accepted the exhortation, but being more diligent, he went to you of his own accord----*NKJV

Paul gives us guidelines on Exhortation in *1 Timothy 6:2--And those who have believing masters, let them not despise them because they are brethren, but rather serve them because those who are benefited are believers and beloved. Teach and exhort these things--NKJV*

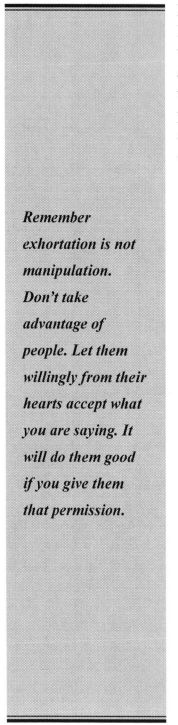

Remember exhortation is not manipulation. Don't take advantage of people. Let them willingly from their hearts accept what you are saying. It will do them good if you give them that permission.

Remember, exhortation is not manipulation. Don't take advantage of people. Let them worship willingly from their hearts and accept what you are saying. It will do them good if you give them that permission. People abhor and reject anyone who imposes himself/herself on others.

Chapter 6

The Tabernacle of David

For most people, the entire concept of Davidic worship is music, dance, praise and adoration of God. But David worship encompassed far more than the rituals surrounding the actual tabernacle. The most important thing was worship from the heart not only from the lips. It's neither the hymns nor the songs, it is the hearts surrendered to God.

As it has been taught in many forums, the Tabernacle of David is divided into three parts. The largest part is the outer court. Found in this court are the brazen lavar and the brazen altar. It is in this place one would repent, purge and wash.

The second largest area is the inner court where one would find the seven candlesticks and the shewbread.

Lastly, the Holies of Holy is the smallest compartment and not many persons enter there. Only the priest with a rope tied around his leg was allowed to enter there. The reason for the rope around his leg is in the event if he was blemished and was struck dead, they were able to pull him out. That is how serious God is about His presence.

We ought to cleanse ourselves before we worship a Holy God.

So worship is important because if I do not have a relationship and a time of intimacy with God, then it means I have nothing really to shout about.

I have to meditate for time of worship.

I have to spend time with God so I can have something to shout about. I would know personally, the God in whom I worship.

Lifting up Holy Hands.

Lifting up of hands is an expression of our reverence to God in worship. It is not a church doctrine. Lifting of hands is a command from the Holy Scriptures. The Bible says, *clap your hands, all you nations; shout to God with cries of joy.*

Psalm 119:48--*I lift up my hands to your commands, which I love, and I meditate on your decrees.* NIV

Lifting of hands is important to you as a believer. Just imagine you have fallen into a ditch and you need someone to help you. The best thing is to raise your hands and the person will lift you easily.

> *So worship is important because if I don't have a relationship and a time of intimacy with God, then it means I have nothing really to shout about.*

- ➤ Lifting up of hands is a sign of love for our God

- ➤ A sign of surrender to him (as in the army)

- ➤ It is a sign of peace and reconciliation

- ➤ It is an acceptance and submission to His authority

> ➤ It is an honor to His person and His name

The Bible says that God has taught our hands to do warfare in the worship. Those that appear before God, whether it is men, women, worshipers and Priest, must purify, cleans and sanctify themselves - free from sin and iniquity. This is holy sacrifice, a holy worship, and the lifting of holy hands.

I reiterate this powerful scripture.

Psalm 24:3-6--*Who may ascend into the hill of the Lord? Or who may stand in His holy place? 4 He who has clean hands and a pure heart,*

Who has not lifted up his soul to an idol, nor sworn deceitfully.

He shall receive blessing from the Lord, and righteousness from the God of his salvation. This is Jacob, the generation of those who seek Him, who seek your face. NKJV

True worshipers of God should not defile themselves. What God wants is genuine worship that comes from the heart and done with clean hands. Anything that brings abomination in the church should be done away with. God's presence is what we need. God's

Anything that brings abomination in the church should be done away with. God's presence is what we need. God's presence removes every burden the devil has put upon our shoulders.

Psalm 95:1-7 says, *Come, let us sing for joy to the Lord; let us shout aloud to the Rock of our salvation. 2 Let us come before him with thanksgiving and extol him with music and song. 3 For the Lord is the great God, the great King above all gods.*

presence removes every burden that the devil has put upon our shoulders. We have the victory in Jesus name. Be assured of what Jesus did on the cross. Sin was dealt with, once and for all. So anything that is abomination, never allow it in your life. God is not pleased by that kind of service.

Read the following scriptures to give you the whole picture of what I am talking about.

Psalm 29:1-2--*Ascribe to the Lord, O mighty ones, ascribe to the Lord glory and strength. Ascribe to the Lord the glory due his name; worship the Lord in the splendor of his holiness.*

The song writer asked, *"what shall I render to you, O Lord? And Holy"*

Speaking by the Holy Spirit, the great Apostle Paul, in advice to the brethren, says in Hebrews 13:15, *'By him therefore, let us offer the sacrifices of Praise to our God continually, that is the fruit of our lips giving thanks to his name.*

In Psalm 22:3, we are given the reason, *'But thou art holy, 0 thou that inhabits the praises of Israel'.*

Our God dwells in the praises of His people in a special way. Praise is part of Worship. Praising is giving glory for what He has done. Is it joyful to lift up His name? God is worthy of our praise and worship. Worship is His habitation. No wonder heaven is a place of joyful worship day and night. The Bible records the worship of thousands of angels, elders and beasts, in an endless manner, worshiping in heaven.

In the same fashion, we are invited to worship the Lord and enter into His gates with thanksgiving and His courts with praise.

Psalm 95:1-7 says, *Come, let us sing for joy to the Lord; let us shout aloud to the Rock of our salvation. 2 Let us come before him with thanksgiving and extol him with music and song. 3 For the Lord is the great God, the great King above all gods. 4 In his hand are the depths of the earth, and the mountain peaks belong to him. 5 The sea is his, for he made it, and his hands formed the dry land. 6 Come, let us bow down in worship, let us kneel before the Lord our Maker; 7 for he is our God and we are the people of his pasture, the flock under his care.* NIV

The vital nature of this invitation and the consideration of the holiness of our God demands serious preparation for qualification to enter His gate and His court.

2 Timothy 2:19-26-*"Nevertheless, God's solid foundation stands firm, sealed with this inscription: "The Lord knows those who are his," and, "Everyone who confesses the name of the Lord must turn away from wickedness. In a large house there are articles not only of gold and silver, but also of wood and clay; some are for noble purposes and some for ignoble. 21 If a man cleanses himself from the latter, he will be an instrument for noble purposes, made holy, useful to the Master and prepared to do any good work.*

By the blood of Jesus, we have access to the throne of God. But we should not take it for granted to do anything we like.

22 Flee the evil desires of youth, and pursue righteousness, faith, love and peace, along with those who call on the Lord out of a pure heart. 23 Don't have anything to do with foolish and stupid arguments, because you know they produce quarrels. 24 And the Lord's servant must not quarrel; instead, he must be kind to everyone, able to teach, not resentful. 25 Those who oppose him he must gently instruct, in the hope that God will grant them repentance leading them to a knowledge of the truth, 26 and that they will come to their senses and escape from the trap of the devil, who has taken them captive to do his will. NIV

By the blood of Jesus, we have access to the throne of God. We should not take it for granted to do anything we like. The Bible says, flee anything that can defile you. There are many things in life that can defile you and render your praise and worship useless or having no impact. No transformation can be seen. Understand God's presence is the guarantee of true change in your life. We are admonished to be holy as He's holy.

Ignorance is expensive

Hosea 4:6, "My people are destroyed from lack of knowledge. Because you have rejected knowledge, I also reject

you as my priests; because you have ignored the law of your God, I also will ignore your children. NIV

This concern is for the novice who are ignorant about true worship and there is a great amount of this in the body of Christ. The enemy uses this weapon to afflict the body. This ignorance has no limit in the body of Christ. It operates from the top to the bottom. That is why knowledge is power.

The devil knows this well and attacks the body mercilessly. Satan deceives person into believing he or she can live any life and it does not matter. Persons dress however and come to the presence of God and it does not matter. They believe one can live in sin at the weekend and on Sunday morning, then come boldly before the awesome and the holy God. The devil make people believe that none of this matters.

What did Satan tell Eve? He deceived her and told her, *"do not mind God, you shall not surely die, the apple is good to the eye, the fashion is good to the eye, I like it, do not mind God."*

But our God loves decency, he expects those that come to His presence to be properly and decently dressed, to appear in a way that gives God honor, an appearance that reflects holiness and humility before Him. Not clothing that reveal body parts which is simply flesh on parade.

Genesis 3:1-7-*Now the serpent was more crafty than any of the wild animals the Lord God had made. He said to the woman, "Did God really say, 'You must not eat from any tree in the garden'?" 2 The woman said to the serpent, "We may eat fruit from the trees in the garden, 3 but God did say, 'You must not eat fruit from the tree that is in the middle of the garden, and you must not touch it, or you will die.'"*

"You will not surely die," the serpent said to the woman. "For God knows that when you eat of it your eyes will be opened, and you

*will be like God, knowing good and evil." 6 When the woman saw that the fruit of the tree was good for food and pleasing to the eye, and also desirable for gaining wisdom, she took some and ate it. She also gave some to her husband, who was with her, and he ate it. 7 Then the eyes of both of them were opened, and they realized they were naked; so they sewed fig leaves together and made coverings for themselves.*NIV

The glorious liberty has been misinterpr-eted as license to indulge in an unacceptable Christian life style. This type of life style glorifies Satan and hurts God.

1 Corinthians 8:9-13, *"Be careful, however, that the exercise of your freedom does not become a stumbling block to the weak. 10 For if anyone with a weak conscience sees you who have this knowledge eating in an idol's temple, won't he be emboldened to eat what has been sacrificed to idols? So this weak brother, for whom Christ died, is destroyed by your knowledge. 12 When you sin against your brothers in this way and wound their weak conscience, you sin against Christ. 13 Therefore, if what I eat causes my brother to fall into sin, I will never eat meat again, so that I will not cause him to fall.* NIV

Other texts to consider Galatians 5:13; 1 Peter 2:16; 2 Corinthians 3:17; Romans 8: 21; Luke 4:8; Isaiah 61:1

Worship is Not Entertainment

Worship is homage rendered to God the Almighty and maker of heaven and earth. This worship should only be made to God and it is not permitted and it is sinful to render it to any other creature or object (idolatry). It is not a group of people or individuals enjoying themselves; it is not an entertainment or an exhibition of singing talent.

Worship is humble; heartfelt Holy Ghost filled rendition of homage and adoration to the Almighty, Omnipotent and Holy God. It is a Holy Ghost empowered, reverential offering or sacrifices in songs, utterances, words, and bodily expression; it is entering God's gates with humble adoration and praise.

Psalm 100--Make a joyful shout to the Lord, all you lands! Serve the Lord with gladness; Come before His presence with singing. Know that the Lord, He is God; It is He who has made us, and not we ourselves; We are His people and the sheep of His pasture.

Enter into His gates with thanksgiving, and into His courts with praise. Be thankful to Him, and bless His name. For the Lord is good; His mercy is everlasting, and His truth endures to all generations--NKJV.

Worship is not entertainment. Worship is homage rendered to God the Almighty and maker of heaven and earth.

It is giving of thanks with all that is within us in songs or praise as a sign of appreciation for the great and many benefits received from God.

When we understand that then worship becomes easy and is our lifestyle. We worship God for who He is and not what He has done. Whether things are good or bad, we worship Him.

Some people think that worship is when life is sweet and on pedestal of glory from one day to another day. That is deception. Sometimes life may be rough and tough. but we should choose to worship God. That is why not all people worship. Worship is for the mature, solid and reliable believers who have a revelation of God's holiness, beauty, wisdom and glory.

It is giving of thanks with all that is within us in songs or praise as a sign of appreciation for the great and many benefits received from God.

See what goes on in Heaven-**Revelation 5:13-14-And every creature which is in heaven and on the earth and under the earth and such as are in the sea, and all that are in them, I heard saying:**

"Blessing and honor and glory and power be to Him who sits on the throne,and to the Lamb, forever and ever!"*

Then the four living creatures said, "Amen!" And the twenty-four elders fell down and worshiped Him who lives forever and ever--NKJV

Chapter 7

Worship Leader

I will give you suggestions that can help the church worship leader to be effective in worship.

Before l move on, remember worship always focuses on God and not the congregation. We bring our hearts to God first and then exhort people to go that path of worship.

Here are the guidelines;

The leader must be familiar with the style of praise and worship of his or her particular church.

1. The leader must be familiar with the style of praise and worship of his or her particular church.

2. A worship leader should be able to unite musicians and congregation rhythmically.

3. The leader must not portray one thing behind the pulpit and another thing the rest of the time. Some people assume a pulpit personality. They live a false lifestyle just in pulpit to impress. Some persons are public success, but private failure. This is very dangerous because people will like you for impressionable ability rather than your spiritual ability.

The worshiper is one who is discipline in himself/herself. A good example is David who profited greatly by his lengthy seasons of solitude. This is an example of discipline.

Psalm 62:5-7--My soul, wait silently for God alone, for my expectation is from Him. He only is my rock and my salvation; He is my defense; I shall not be moved.

In God is my salvation and my glory; the rock of my strength, and my refuge, is in God--NKJV

From such disciplines, David led others into sweet worship. He was a good worshiper. God found a place in the heart of David. This discipline helped David to perfect his musical skills.

We can emulate from David's lifestyle if we want to move higher into worship.

Qualifications of Worship Leader and his Team

I would give you the qualifications of a Worship Leader and the worship team which I believe will assist the church to go further in the things of God.

1. Must be a worshiper from the heart.
2. A deep and a prone spiritual walk (2Timothy 5:10)
3. The leader must be musically inclined to an acceptable level.
4. The leader must be able to function as part of a team.
5. The leader must have a proper attitude towards the church, pastor, and church doctrine.
6. The leader must be willing to commit himself to this position, sacrificing prerogative to visit.
7. The leader must have an enthusiastic, friendly and warm personality.
8. The dress code is very important. Worship time is not an opportunity for flesh to be on parade.
9. Worshipers should be punctual for worship service. All worship team members showing up late will affect the experience and set a bad example in the audience for the

duration of the service. It is just respect and reverence for the house of God.

10. Know the Word of God and be a person given to much prayer.

> *Worshipers should be punctual for worship service. All worship team members showing up late will affect and set a bad example in the audience for the duration of the service.*

Chapter 8

The Art of Leading Worship

David was of the greatest kings who ever lived because he was a true worshiper. He had limitations and inadequacies in life, but he loved God. He did not allow anything to stop him from the place of worship.

1. David was a worshiper
2. David worshiped publicly
3. David worshiped inwardly
4. David worshiped lovingly
5. David worshiped enthusiastically
6. David worshiped defensively
7. David worshiped lavishly
8. David worshiped actively
9. David worshiped obediently
10. David worshiped joyfully
11. David worshiped righteously
12. David worshiped repentantly
13. David worshiped quietly
14. David worshiped repeatedly
15. David worshiped encouragingly
16. David worshiped by giving sacrifices
17. David worshiped God by forgiving others
18. David worshiped when he was elderly

David worshiped the true and living God. God said, "I have found a man after my own heart". Why did God say so? David was a true worshiper.

Who we worship depends on what kind of life style we will portray.

I said you become based on the God (god) you worship.

Psalm 115:8--Those who make them are like them; so is everyone who trusts in them—NKJV

Your life is measured by the kind of God (god) you worship. Some people worship others, some worship money, some worship material things, some worship pleasures of the world and there are those who worship the true God. The choice is yours. I suggest you let God, the creator of heavens and the earth, receive your true worship.

Your life is measured by the kind of God (god) you worship. Some people worship others, some worship money, some material things, some worship pleasures of the world and there are those who worship the true God.

Guidelines of leading worship

i.   The worship leader should be born again and filled with the Spirit of God. The Holy Spirit is the best teacher and knows the mind of God. Allow the Spirit to guide you.

ii. The word of God should be imperative. The worship leader goes into depth of worship to the level of his/her understanding of the word of God. The Spirit guides you based on the word.

iii. Personal prayer life. You can only worship the God you know. Prayer develops your intimacy with the Lord.

iv. Desire, determine and discipline yourself to live a pure life. Sin dilutes worship. Who you are is transferred to the congregation. Guard your heart from sin and any other contaminations-Proverbs 4:23.

v. Practice-Let worship be your lifestyle. Some people worship only in the church. When they come out, it stops there. That should not be the case. Worship is God's nature in us and so consistency is the watchword.

Chapter 9

Worship and Warfare

One of the tricks of the enemy to frustrate the church is through lies and deception. His threefold mission as shown by Christ in **John 10:10**, to kill, steal and destroy are cultivated through lies. When the enemy speaks, do not buy in and accept his words. Hidden in his voice is a trap to deny you your rights in Christ. Thank God the truth is here that we are victorious inspite of what we go through. We are not evaluated by circumstances of life, but what Christ did on the cross.

That is why spiritual warfare is real. You can not shut your eyes and pretend there is nothing of that sort. The devil plays with your ignorance and he will make sure you stay there in darkness.

Apostle Paul opened the eyes of Ephesian church to see the nature of warfare.

> *When the enemy speaks, do not buy in and accept his words. Hidden in his voice is a trap to deny you your rights in Christ. Thank God the truth is here that we are victorious inspite of what we go through.*

Finally, my brethren, be strong in the Lord, and in the power of his might. Put on the whole armour of God, that ye may be able to stand against the wiles of the devil. For we wrestle not against flesh and blood, but against principalities, against powers, against the rulers of the darkness of this world, against spiritual wickedness in high [places].

Wherefore take unto you the whole armour of God, that ye may be able to withstand in the evil day, and having done all, to stand. Stand therefore, having your loins girt about with truth, and having on the breastplate of righteousness; And your feet shod with the preparation of the gospel of peace; Above all, taking the shield of faith, wherewith ye shall be able to quench all the fiery darts of the wicked-- Ephesians 6:10-16, KJV

That is why it's important to engage in spiritual warfare with sufficient knowledge. Having the right information cuts any spiritual warfare to size. Remember, you cannot defeat the enemy that you do not know. Beware of the schemes of the devil and the available weapons at your disposal to finish the job well without any casualty.

And of the children of Issachar, [which were men] that had understanding of the times, to know what Israel ought to do; the heads of them [were] two hundred; and all their brethren [were] at their commandment.(KJV),I Chronicles 12:32

Whatever you know determines how far you will go. New information gives you advancement in life. Knowledge of the enemy makes the battle easier.

I want to say here before you engage the enemy in battle, learn to worship. When you worship, you surrender to God who fights your battles. Our warfare is not carnal, but spiritual. That is why we need the word of God and Holy Spirit to guide us in this matter.

Psalm 8:2 Out of the mouth of babes and nursing infants You have ordained strength (praise), Because of Your enemies, That You may silence the enemy and the avenger. The praise of a believer is so powerful. God has ordained the praise to still the avenger or to paralyze the enemy from advancing your life. This type of praise sends the enemy into confusion because he can not understand how you can praise considering all the trouble that is in your life. You are bombarded left, right and center, but yet, you praise your God. The enemy must now go back in his chamber and strategize again how to discourage you from trusting God.

You can't go into battle using your physical strength and power.

Proverbs 24:6--For by wise counsel you will wage your own war, and in a multitude of counselors there is safety--NKJV

In the Bible, there are plenty of testimonies of people who fell down into worship before entering the battlefield. I will give you a few examples why worship is powerful.

Whatever you know determines how far you will go.

New information gives you advancement in life.

Knowledge of the enemy makes the battle easier.

JOSHUA

Joshua 5:14-15--So He said, "No, but as Commander of the army of the Lord I have now come."

And Joshua fell on his face to the earth and worshiped, and said to Him, "What does my Lord say to His servant?"

Then the Commander of the LORD's army said to Joshua,"Take your sandal off your foot, for the place where you stand is holy." And Joshua did so--NKJV

KING JEHOSHOPHAT

2 Chronicles 20:18-19--And Jehoshaphat bowed his head with his face to the ground, and all Judah and the inhabitants of Jerusalem bowed before the LORD, worshiping the LORD--NKJV

Chapter 10

♥

The Mystery of Praise
and Thanksgiving

I want to begin by saying praise and thanksgiving is part of worship. We praise and thank God who has been revealed to us. Our hearts have been touched and influenced by His presence. Therefore we yearn, desire and pursue God through praise and thanksgiving for the wonderful things He has done for us.

The Power of Praise

> *There is power in praise. That is why God inhabits in the praises of His people (Psalm 22:3). Every human loves praise.*

There is power in praise. That is why God inhabits the praises of His people (Psalm 22:3). Every human loves praise. People are normally attracted where they are praised and avoid any element of intimidation. Look at any leader whether it be a pastor, a president or even the local leader, he or she will join any singing group that talks about him in song and dance. **Praise is the key to invite God's presence.** Remember, the devil can never withstand powerful praises. It chokes and suffocates him. That is why sorrow, murmuring, anxiety and feelings of hopelessness create a good environment for the devil to reign. He loves such a place, because he knows God cannot be found there. As a believer, you have an obligation to maintain your joy at all costs. However, the situation maybe, you can never afford to lose your joy.

Apostle James saw the importance of joy to a believer. James 5:13-14

"Is any one of you in trouble? He should pray. Is anyone happy? Let him sing songs of praise"-NIV

When you sing or praise out of a joyful heart, it is acceptable before God. Do not allow sorrow or grumbling to deny you your place in God's presence. One of the reasons that stopped the children of Israel to reach their promised land was murmuring. They did not have joy in serving God. They saw it as a burden that they could not carry. But God saw their attitude and denied them that opportunity to possess Canaan. Caleb and Joshua had the right attitude. God was faithful to give them their inheritance in the land of Canaan.

'Consider it pure joy, my brothers, whenever you face trials of many kinds, 3 because you know that the testing of your faith develops perseverance.

Perseverance must finish its work so that you may be mature and complete, not lacking anything.

James 1:2-8--*'Consider it pure joy, my brothers, whenever you face trials of many kinds, 3 because you know that the testing of your faith develops perseverance. 4 Perseverance must finish its work so that you may be mature and complete, not lacking anything. 5 If any of you lacks wisdom, he should ask God, who gives generously to all without finding fault, and it will be given to him. 6 But when he asks, he must believe and not doubt, because he who doubts is like a wave of the sea, blown and tossed by the wind. 7 That man should not think he will receive anything from the Lord; 8 he is a double-minded man, unstable in all he does. NIV*

No matter how things may be, never throw away your joy. Joy is an expectation that something good will come forth. People may change

Kateryann Johnson, CPA, CGMA, CFF

and leave you alone. Situation may change also, but you need to maintain your joy at all cost. Your praise and worship is acceptable in the environment of joy. Is there anything bothering you? Maintain your joy. Are you down in the valley of defeat and loss? Let your joy in the Lord lift you up in victory.

Look at this scenario in the book of 2 Chronicles 20:20-23

> *No matter things may be, never throw away your joy. Joy is an expectation that something good will come forth. People may change and leave you alone.*

Early in the morning they left for the Desert of Tekoa. As they set out, Jehoshaphat stood and said, "Listen to me, Judah and people of Jerusalem! Have faith in the Lord your God and you will be upheld; have faith in his prophets and you will be successful." 21 After consulting the people, Jehoshaphat appointed men to sing to the Lord and to praise him for the splendor of his holiness as they went out at the head of the army, saying:

"Give thanks to the Lord, for his love endures forever."

As they began to sing and praise, the Lord set ambushes against the men of Ammon and Moab and Mount Seir who were invading Judah, and they were defeated. 23 The men of Ammon and Moab rose up against the men from Mount Seir to destroy and humiliate them. After they finished slaughtering the men from Seir, they helped to destroy one another. When the men of Judah came to the place that overlooks the desert and looked toward the vast army, they saw only dead bodies lying on the ground; no one had escaped. 25 So Jehoshaphat and his men went to carry off their plunder, and they found among them a great amount of equipment and clothing and also articles of value — more than they could take

48

away. There was so much plunder that it took three days to collect it. 26 On the fourth day they assembled in the Valley of Beracah, where they praised the Lord. This is why it is called the Valley of Beracah to this day. 27 Then, led by Jehoshaphat, all the men of Judah and Jerusalem returned joyfully to Jerusalem, for the Lord had given them cause to rejoice over their enemies. 28 They entered Jerusalem and went to the temple of the Lord with harps and flutes and trumpets. NIV

King Jehoshaphat and the entire Nation of Israel were outnumbered as far as the battle was concerned. They were expecting a severe defeat and shame by their enemy. God released a word through a prophet and they obeyed. They went to battle singing unto the Lord. God defeated the enemy on their behalf.

Joy is the key to your victory. Celebrate the goodness of the Lord.

Praise can defined in the following ways.

> *Joy is the key to your victory. Celebrate the goodness of the Lord.*

It is to produce clear sound in this towards God with a purpose.

To celebrate and boast in God's glory.

In praise, there must be no confusion to what is intended. Praise is important. God loves to be praised.

- **Hilluwi** - Praise can be expressed as a celebration of thanksgiving for a successful completion of harvest. This may include singing and dancing.

- **Tehillah** - Singing and celebrating is giving clear songs and boasting to God.

- **Shabach** - Praise can be a shout, done with a loud voice and shout of a triumph in glorifying God's victory. Psalms 47:1.

- **Zamar** - Praise can be expressed by using musical instruments in accompaniment.

- **Towallah** - Praise is an act of singing and celebrating in extension of hands in adoration and thanksgiving.

It can also be seen as to speak well of, to express admiration for, to commend, to congratulate.

Don't forget God loves your praise. You attract him by your praise. Never murmur or complain. It shuts off the power and the presence of God.

Why Thanksgiving?

God has done so many things for you. Why can't you take some time and thank him for His goodness? Many believers know how to praise and worship, but thanksgiving is hard to come from their lips. They have the spirit of murmuring always. Something small happens to their life and they begin to murmur a lot. I wrote this book for you so that you may learn how to thank God. What has God done for you? Learn to celebrate Him. Take your time and dance in your living room.

"Thanksgiving" as a word appear in the Bible so many times. It is the highest form of our gratitude to God.

Thanksgiving by definition is the act of giving thanks or expressing gratitude for favors or mercy received.

> *Thanksgiving as a word appear in the Bible so many times. It is the highest form of our gratitude to God. Thanksgiving is the act of giving thanks or expressing gratitude for favors or mercy received.*

Kateryann Johnson, CPA, CGMA, CFF

Psalm 100:4-*"Enter into his gates with thanksgiving"*

Thanksgiving gives us access into God's habitation and strong places.

To be thankful is to act and respond with a heart of gratitude after God has blessed you.

Psalm 103 says, *"Bless the Lord oh my soul and all that s within me, bless the Lord, o my soul and forget not all His benefits.*

Who forgives all your iniquities who heals all your diseases.

Who redeems your life from destruction.

Who crowns you with loving kindness and tender mercies.

Who satisfies your mount with good things so that your youth is renewed like the eagles.

> *Thanksgiving gives us access into God's habitation and strong places.*
>
> *To be thankful is to act and respond with a heart of gratitude after God has blessed you.*

THE POWER OF THANKSGIVING

(i) Thanksgiving confuses the enemy. He does not understand when you praise and thank God inspite of situation you are going through.

(ii) Thanksgiving keeps your heart pure. You divorce bitterness through thanksgiving.

(iii) Thanksgiving activates the rivers within you that quenches your thirst inspite of the pain around you.

(iv) Thanksgiving maintains victory. It is the lubricant of my spirit, soul and body.

(v) Thanksgiving is the staircase to my destiny. A thankless heart increases pain.

(vi) Thanksgiving triggers grace in the season I am going through.

To live a fulfilled life, you need to be grateful with every little thing God does for you. Never take anything for granted. The children of Israel did not see the promise land because they murmured against God except Caleb and Joshua.

Numbers 14:20-25--*The Lord replied, "I have forgiven them, as you asked. 21 Nevertheless, as surely as I live and as surely as the glory of the Lord fills the whole earth, 22 not one of the men who saw my glory and the miraculous signs I performed in Egypt and in the desert but who disobeyed me and tested me ten times — 23 not one of them will ever see the land I promised on oath to their forefathers. No one who has treated me with contempt will ever see it. 24 But because my servant Caleb has a different spirit and follows me wholeheartedly, I will bring him into the land he went to, and his descendants will inherit it. 25 Since the Amalekites and Canaanites are living in the valleys, turn back tomorrow and set out toward the desert along the route to the Red Sea."* **NIV**

Murmuring and complaining is sin before God. It is a sign of unbelief.

God had delivered the children of Israel from bondage in Egypt by miracles and wonders through the hand of Moses. On the way to the Promise Land, they forgot the works of God and then began to murmur. They complained a lot against Moses for their predicaments in the wilderness. God was not happy with that.

Murmuring and complaining is sin before God. It is a sign of unbelief-why am I suffering? Why am I not married? Why am I poor?

When you begin to question the integrity of God, you lose your place in Him. You miss your blessings and favor.

Like the children of Israel, you will be stagnated in your walk with God.

Murmuring takes you back and can destroy you if you are not careful.

The key to deal with any kind of murmuring is to be grateful. Thank God for your life.

- Thank God that you have an opportunity to progress because of His presence.

- Be grateful over your children.

- Thank God from your heart that you are a candidate for marriage.

- Thank God for your business, though it may be small but it has potential to become world-wide enterprise.

- Thank God for your house of worship.

You have a reason to thank God for, because you cannot manage your life single handedly. There is power in giving God thanks. Remember, prayer is powerful when it is accompanied with thanksgiving.

Philippians 4:6-7--Be anxious for nothing, but in everything by prayer and supplication, with thanksgiving, let your requests be made known to God; 7 and the peace of God, which surpasses all understanding, will guard your hearts and minds through Christ Jesus--*NKJV*

I have seen some believers praying ceaselessly, but when you check their life, they do not have any results. They are bitter, envious and engage in murmuring because they see their friends having progressed and they seem to be left behind. To them God is not fair. Why this and why that? This is the reason for their murmuring and complaining.

God does not want you to take that path. Be grateful in your heart. God is faithful to intervene on your behalf. Have faith in Him and allow him to work for you. Murmuring will not help you. The devil will use that spirit of murmuring to fight you.

I want you to learn the secret of giving God thanks. Thanksgiving is the medicine against murmuring and bitterness. When you develop that lifestyle of appreciating God's grace, He gives you the power to triumph and live above the attacks of the enemy. The devil cannot survive the realms of praise and thanksgiving. It suffocates him.

The way to His presence is praise and worship which culminates into thanksgiving.

> *I want you to learn the secret of giving God thanks. Thanksgiving is the medicine against murmuring and bitterness. When you develop that lifestyle of appreciating God's grace, He gives you the power to triumph and live above the attacks of the enemy.*

Psalm 50:14-15--Offer to God thanksgiving, and pay your vows to the Most High. Call upon Me in the day of trouble; I will deliver you, and you shall glorify Me." -NKJV

Kateryann Johnson, CPA, CGMA, CFF

God gives us all things to worship Him. Never forget that. Put that at the bottom of your heart and it will go well with you.

There is power in praise, worship and giving of thanks to our God.

Take that position and see your life being transformed.

Conclusion

There are benefits in worship.

People make time for what is important.

People want to get something out of their worship experience that they are not getting anywhere else.

Real worship is a lot more than attending weekly meetings. Worship is where we allow the supernatural God of the Bible to show up and to interact with people in the pews.

The Lord should always be in the central focus of worship not just a visitor in the back row.

Are you born again? Worship is for those who know Christ personally.

You may love the Lord and give offerings at the church, but you don't know Him personally.

I am here to help you see things in the right perspective. God calls us to worship Him in season and out of season. That is why being filled by His Sprit is imperative.

The question is, has Jesus forgiven you all your sins? That is important. True worship is by the Spirit and is sustained in the same manner.

I have seen people going to church, they are committed and do a lot then they cease to continue. What was done in the flesh cannot please God. You need to be born again. It is only Him who can help you, keep you on the track and renew you when challenging moments come.

This is the way to enter that place of true worship. This is the start of obtaining the heart of a worshiper.

Confess this prayer,

Lord Jesus, I acknowledge my sins and repent of them. I believe I cannot save myself and therefore I permit you to forgive me all my sins and wash me by your precious blood. Come into my heart and keep me by your grace. Thank you, Lord, for saving me. I am now born again. Help me to worship you in spirit and in truth. I pray in Jesus name-Amen.

> *I am here to help you see things in the right perspective. God calls us to worship Him in season and out of season. That is why being filled by His Sprit is imperative.*

Printed in the United States
By Bookmasters